THE POLITICAL
DISCIPLE

ORDINARY THEOLOGY SERIES

THE POLITICAL DISCIPLE

A THEOLOGY OF
PUBLIC LIFE

VINCENT BACOTE

GENE L. GREEN, SERIES EDITOR

ZONDERVAN

The Political Disciple
Copyright © 2015 by Vincent Bacote

This title is also available as a Zondervan ebook.
Visit www.zondervan.com/ebooks.

Requests for information should be addressed to:

Zondervan, 3900 *Sparks Dr. SE, Grand Rapids, Michigan 49546*

Library of Congress Cataloging-in-Publication Data

Bacote, Vincent, 1965–
    The political disciple : a theology of public life / Vincent Bacote.
        pages cm — (Ordinary theology)
    ISBN 978-0-310-51607-1 (softcover)
    1. Christianity and politics. 2. Christian leadership. 3. Political
participation. 4. Public officers. I. Title.
    BR115.P7B1426   2015
    261.7 — dc23

Cover design: Micah Kandros
Interior design: Beth Shagene
Editorial: Madison Trammel, Lauren Niswonger, Bob Hudson

Printed in the United States of America

15 16 17 18 19 20 21 22 23 24 25 /DCI/ 14 13 12 11 10 9 8 7 6 5 4 3 2 1

For my wife, Shelley,
and our two daughters,
who lovingly support me
as I pursue God's call on my life.

CONTENTS

FOREWORD TO THE ORDINARY THEOLOGY SERIES

GENE L. GREEN

ORDINARY THEOLOGY. THESE TWO WORDS TOGETHER sound like an oxymoron. We're accustomed to thinking about "theology" as the stiff and stifling stuff found in ponderous tomes written by Christian scholars in ivory towers, places far removed from our ordinary lives. We live on the street, in our homes, in places of business, in schools, in gyms, and in churches. What does theology have to do with the ordinary affairs of our daily lives?

We want to bring the Bible into our lives, to be sure, and we attend church to learn about God's Word. We read our favorite passages and wonder how ancient stories about Noah on the water or Jesus on the water relate to the checkout at the grocery store, the hours at work, the novel we read for pleasure, the sicknesses we endure, the votes we cast, or the bed. How do we construct a bridge between the biblical worlds and the twenty-first-century world as we seek to follow Jesus faithfully? The distance between our local shopping center and Paul's forum in Athens (Acts 17) seems like an unbridgeable canyon. What does the Bible have to do with the wonderful or difficult realities we face on the baseball field or in the city? How do we receive God's Word, which is truly for all people, at all times, in all places?

It's an old question, one the church has been asking for centuries. The Bible is a historical document with contemporary relevance. But we're also aware that it doesn't seem to speak directly to many situations we face. There is no obvious biblical view of nuclear war, a kind of destruction unknown in the ancient world. What about epidemics such as AIDS, an unknown disease in the ancient world? The Noah story describes a dramatic climate change, but does that cataclysm have anything to do with global warming today? Through the centuries, Christians have understood that the Bible cannot be simply proof-texted in all life's situations. Yet we still believe that the Bible is God's word for us in our complex world. Enter theology.

The word *theology* comes from a couple of Greek terms: *theos* and *logos*. *Theos* means "God" and *logos* means "word." Simply stated, theology is words that express thoughts about God. We hold beliefs about God such as "God is love" (1 John 4:8). We understand that Jesus died for our sins and that we have a hope that transcends the grave because of the resurrection of Christ. All these are theological statements. We have received Christian theology through our parents, church, and Scripture reading, and we attempt to find how biblically based belief relates to our lives. We do theology as we take Scripture and our inherited theology and seek to work out what God is saying about the issues of today. Every Christian is a theologian.

Ordinary theology is, really, just another way to say *theol-*

ogy. The expression emphasizes how theology is part of the ordinary stuff of daily life. Food is a theological topic. We can think about buying food, the need for food, those without food, selling food. What does the Bible have to say about food supply, hunger, and generosity? To ask that question is to think theologically about food. What about government welfare or foreign aid? We can think through the whole of Scripture and apply its perspectives and teachings to such issues. This is theology. And it is something every Christian can and must do. We believe that the gospel is relevant not only to our inner life, but to life in the world. The road we travel as ordinary Christians is to do "ordinary theology" as we work God's message into all aspects of daily life.

The Ordinary Theology Series has a few goals. The first is to take up the common issues of daily life and think through them theologically. But another purpose of the series is to invite you to develop your skills as a theologian. These small books are examples of theological method but also a welcome into the necessary, challenging, and joyous task of doing theology. We're all called to follow the example of the first great Christian theologian whose day job was netting fish for a living. Peter did not receive training in the rabbinic schools as had Paul, yet he was the one who first understood and stated that Jesus was the Christ, the Son of the Living God (Matthew 16:16). He also opened the door of faith to the Gentiles as he came to understand that God accepts every person, regardless of ethnicity (Acts 10). Each of us can make a theological contribution to the church, our family, our community, and our own life. For your sake and the sake of others, be a theologian.

One final word about format. Each chapter begins with a story, and theological reflection follows. Theology happens in the place where Scripture meets us on the road where "life is lived tensely, where thought has its birth in conflict and concern, where choices are made and decisions are carried out."[1] We go to Scripture and the deep well of Christian theology as we develop our theology in the place where we find ourselves. God is concerned about people and places and does not ask us to divorce ourselves from them as we follow and serve Christ. And he gives us guidance on how to do that. So, enjoy the read! And again: be the theologian.

PROLOGUE

YOU NEVER KNOW WHAT MIGHT HAPPEN WHEN YOU GO TO the store on an errand. In the summer of 2012, I was minding my own business in the Whole Foods Market in Wheaton, Illinois, when my colleague Gene Green came up to me and said, "Vince, would you like to write a short book on political theology for a series I'm putting together?" Before I knew it, the word *yes* came out of my mouth. Although I had thought about writing other books on related topics, and though I had taught many courses on political theology, it never occurred to me to write about it until that conversation.

But this book is not a survey of political theology like the ones I assign to my students. There are already many good books out there, such as Elizabeth Phillips's recent *Political Theology: A Guide for the Perplexed* (London: T & T Clark, 2012). So what am I doing in this brief volume?

First, we need to be clear about what we mean by *political theology*. If you survey a number of books, articles, and blogs, you will discover that it can mean several things. It can be any of the following:

1. An academic discussion of the ways faith and politics intersect

2. A consideration of what the Bible says about politics
3. An examination of political life in a particular context and interpreting it through a biblical/theological lens
4. A survey of Christians who have been involved in politics
5. A survey of Christian traditions that have had some kind of political involvement

The list could go on, but even those five approaches help us to see that the terrain is vast. The territory is sometimes covered under the label *theology of public life* and at other times under the label *public theology*. What's the difference? *Theology of public life* refers to the ways a person uses the discipline of theology as a lens to view various topics related to the public domain. *Public theology* covers the same topics but also considers how a person would bring theological ideas into the public realm, and sometimes how these theological ideas translate (or are unable to translate) into publicly accessible language.

So what does *political theology* mean? In these pages, it refers to the consideration of Christian discipleship in the public domain with an emphasis on political life (in a broad sense). To put it another way, the big question I am trying to answer is: Can there be Christian faithfulness in the public realm? If politics refers to our lives as citizens, then what does it mean to be Christian and a citizen of a county, state, country, or world? To answer this requires us to consider other questions like these:

- Should Christians even participate in the public sphere?
- How might Christian beliefs influence our engagement in the public realm?
- How should Christians understand their identity?

- What kind of people should Christians be in public?
- How might Christians retain hope, given the frustrations of public engagement?

Though each question deserves a book of its own, this volume will examine various facets of these inquiries. These four chapters and the postscript will, I hope, serve as catalysts for a further examination of the way our faith relates to the public realm. I pray that this book will lead to many fruitful discussions and to a deeper Christian faith.

1

PERMISSION:
CAN WE GO OUT IN PUBLIC?

A T VARIOUS TIMES IN MY YOUTH AND YOUNG ADULTHOOD I found myself heavily influenced by my peers and superiors, especially when they stated strong opinions, whether it was about sports, music, politics, or faith. It's not that I didn't have a mind of my own, but I had a strong desire to know the right way to think about things. As I grew in my faith during my college years, I was particularly attentive to ways that spiritual leaders expressed their views on the priorities that should be most important for Christians. While I had my own thoughts, I was willing to listen to the views of the spiritual leaders I heard in church and at conferences.

When it came to the question of how a Christian should think about life in the public realm, as I discovered that there were strong opinions across a wide spectrum, my eagerness to find the right answer became a challenge. Only later did I recognize that my college years coincided with a time when evangelical Christians were sorting out how much priority they should give to matters of public life.

Looking back on my evangelical sojourn over the past three

decades, I have seen many committed believers reach different conclusions about Christian engagement in the public realm, especially when *public* is synonymous with *political*. Many questions are tied to this: How are we to make the most of the days allotted to us in a way that will please God? Is it a waste of time to invest our lives in the messiness that comes with public life? Or to put it more strongly, Can a Christian live a life of faithfulness and also involve oneself in the political arena? Evangelicals have wrestled with these questions for quite some time.

Although the Jerry Falwell – led Moral Majority (1979 – 89)* was influential in encouraging Christian political engagement, significant ambivalence remained among evangelicals when I entered divinity school in 1990. This ambivalence about Christian engagement, or in some cases resistance to it, was prominently displayed in the differing views about the relationship of Christian mission and social action. While some readers may point to Carl F. H. Henry's *The Uneasy Conscience of Modern Fundamentalism* (1947) or the Lausanne Covenant's articulation of the gospel in 1974, neither of these important signposts resulted in a sweeping consensual view that Christians should be engaged in the world or link social and political engagement to gospel mission.

In one of my classes, we invited a missions professor to discuss the question of mission and social action. While he suggested that it was important for Christians to care about

---

* The Moral Majority was an organization associated with the Christian Right that was one of the most high-profile conservative Christian political organizations. It was formed to facilitate conservative Christian engagement in the political process. For some, it is ironic that Falwell, a fundamentalist Baptist, was the leader of a political organization. Upon its dissolution in 1989, Falwell was content that the Christian Right was sufficiently established politically.

a broad range of social concerns, it was also clear that he was nervous about making too close a link between gospel and the broad domain of social, cultural, and political life. The fear was that if the link became too close, then the social gospel (a term most associated with Walter Rauschenbusch) would creep in and change the message to one that eliminated spiritual and eternal concerns and restated the gospel as merely an earthly salvation that addressed such issues as poverty and politics. There might also have been a fear of liberation theology, which was more overtly political and critical of Western capitalist societies.

Though this was only one example of how some Christians were ambivalent about Christian public engagement, it is important to qualify it by saying that there was fairly consistent public moral concern about issues like abortion, though this moral concern did not translate consistently into public engagement beyond an encouragement to vote.

The circumstances I encountered during my divinity-school years changed fairly dramatically by the end of the 1990s. By then, many evangelicals were talking about a holistic faith that expressed concern for society as well as for souls, ultimately reaching a peak in the early years of George W. Bush's presidency. Initially, the Bush White House was regarded as an environment where evangelicals could have public influence, most notably in terms of the Faith-Based Initiative and the role of Wheaton College alumnus Michael Gerson* as a presidential speechwriter. Yet by 2002, media reports began to indicate that younger adult evangelicals were getting excited about a

---

* Michael Gerson is currently a columnist for the *Washington Post* and a fellow for both the ONE Campaign and the Center for Public Justice. He was the chief speechwriter for President George W. Bush from 2001 to 2006.

holistic faith but wanted to change the tone and turn the focus away from the Religious Right, which had been prominent in evangelical politics at least since the 1970s. These younger Christians wanted the prominent issues to expand beyond abortion and gay marriage to include issues like the environment and poverty. This desire remains, but not without being contested in some circles.

By the time of the 2008 election, weariness from the Iraq war along with frustration with the minimal gains from political activity yielded an evangelical populace that had a new ambivalence, a buyer's remorse about politics. Many evangelicals did not wish to disengage but were now wondering where the best place was to apply their efforts. The value of political action once again became, and remains, an open question.

One other notable factor contributed to this ambivalence: the lack of a strong theological basis for Christian involvement in the political sphere, and that is despite the fact that nearly a decade had passed since a great majority of evangelicals concluded that a holistic, publicly engaged gospel was simply common sense. This dearth of theological underpinning is one of the main reasons for this book.

Moving Beyond Intuition to Conviction

It may seem a stretch, but the question of evangelical engagement in politics is similar to the question of whether Christians have good reason to participate in secular culture generally — in film and music, for example. My experience of finding a culture-affirming Christianity runs a parallel path to my experience of thinking about whether Christians should take seriously the issue of political theology.

The central question of this initial chapter is one of permission: Are Christians even *allowed* to participate in the public sphere? To put it differently, do Christians have either direct commands or indirect imperatives that permit, demand, or make optional some form of participation in public life? This was not an easy question for me years ago, and it remains a difficult one for many Christians today. Ultimately, I arrived at my answer through the doctrine of creation. How did this happen?

It happened because I fantasized about being a rock star. Actors and actresses often intrigued me, but I never wanted to be like them. Instead, I wanted to be up there on stage, and, depending upon the particular fantasy, playing the role of the lead singer or the bassist or the lead guitarist. My fantasy was about the fun of being a performer who goes on tour and plays for large audiences all over the world. My love of rock music and my commitment to Christ, however, resulted in this crisis: How is it possible to affirm "the world" and put God first? This question is fundamental to public engagements, whether social, cultural, educational, or political.

In college and the years immediately afterward, I only had a hunch that it was God-honoring and theologically valid to appreciate the good things that emerged from the culture external to the church, and that it was "Christianly sensible" to work toward improving society culturally and politically. I had no theological categories or biblical texts to support my view, but I had a sense that one could be Christian while appreciating and participating in the surrounding culture.

I began to move beyond the level of intuition about a year or two before I went to seminary because of my exposure to the work of Francis Schaeffer. The film series *How Then Shall We*

Live was my first exposure to a Christian leader who thought we should live in God's world in a way indicative of a desire to transform the culture while also expressing appreciation for the good things in the broader culture. It was a relief to learn that there were Christians whose response to the culture was neither exclusively evangelistic nor escapist.

Although I was encouraged by Schaeffer's example, I still lacked a theological argument for why Christians could appreciate and engage the culture. Not until my years in divinity school did I finally find a theological voice for my long-held intuition.

I entered Trinity Evangelical Divinity School intending to prepare for pastoral ministry and hoping to discover some way to demonstrate that Christians should engage the culture. Within the first year, I was on a path toward greater clarity in my vocation (as a professor rather than a pastor) and was hoping to find time in my schedule to study the relationship between theology and culture. In my spare time I began to research authors who had written on this topic. I discovered that many people referred to Abraham Kuyper as an important figure in this discussion, and I was sufficiently intrigued to do an independent study of his theology of culture. A door was opening to a world that would begin to supply theological substance to my intuition about Christian cultural engagement.

First, a disclaimer: Every theologian is a human being with flaws. I learned this early while reading Kuyper. Like many of his time, he made assumptions about civilization and race, namely, that Europeans were superior to other people, especially those with African heritage. My encounter with Kuyper's statements on race led me to become a critical thinker. I had to decide whether it was possible to find helpful aspects of his theology when I knew that he regarded someone like me as inferior. As I thought about it, it became clear that his views on race actually contradicted the best aspects of this theology. Kuyper could not transcend his own cultural biases and completely live up to the implications of his theology. I learned that even the greatest figures have feet of clay. Still, I label myself "Kuyperian" in spite of the troubling deficiencies of the man himself. And I think that he now, in heaven, has a more accurate view of things.

My study on Kuyper's theology of culture focused primarily on his L. P. Stone Lectures delivered at Princeton Seminary in 1898. As I read the first lecture I came across a quotation that was inspiring, invigorating, and ultimately life changing. Kuyper states that Calvinism

> ... has not only honored *man* for the sake of his likeness to
> the Divine image, but also *the world* as a Divine creation,
> and has at once placed to the front the great principle that
> there is a *particular grace* which works Salvation, and also
> a *common grace* by which God, maintaining the life of the
> world, relaxes the curse which rests upon it, arrests its
> process of corruption, and thus allows the untrammeled
> development of our life in which to glorify Himself as Cre-
> ator. Thus the Church receded in order to be neither more
> nor less than the congregation of believers, and in every
> department the life of the world was not emancipated
> from God, but from the dominion of the Church. Thus
> domestic life regained its independence, trade and com-
> merce realized their strength in liberty, art and science
> were set free from every ecclesiastical bond and restored
> to their own inspirations, and man began to understand
> the subjection of all nature with its hidden forces and
> treasures to himself as a holy duty, imposed upon him by

the original ordinances of Paradise: "Have dominion over them." Henceforth the curse should no longer rest upon the world itself, but upon that which is sinful in it, and instead of monastic flight from the world the duty is now emphasized of serving God in the world, in every position in life. To praise God in the Church and serve Him in the world became the inspiring impulse, and, in the Church, strength was to be gathered by which to resist temptation and sin in the world ... the life of the world is to be honored in its independence ... we must, in every domain, discover the treasures and develop the potencies hidden by God in nature and in human life."[2]

As I have written elsewhere, these words were like oxygen to me.[3] I had been gasping for air for years, sustained by a faint intuition in what seemed like a theological vacuum. No longer. At last I had found a theological affirmation for Christian engagement in the world. This discovery gave my Christian faith a language that was new to me.

The most important aspect of this thrilling discovery was the doctrine of common grace. I had never seen the words *common* and *grace* together; I had understood *grace* to refer primarily to God's unmerited favor toward us in the salvation that comes through Christ. Now I was reading about a grace of creation that made it possible for us to bring God glory by our participation in the world. I had sensed in the past that there was a theological argument for this stance, and now I discovered that it had a name. Common grace was the key to a deeper theology of creation and the reason for taking life "in the world" seriously. I was now on a path to an informed faith that would wed the lordship of Christ to my desire to affirm our embrace of the public aspects of life.

Not Quite Worldly

Another phrase that leaped out at me as I read this passage again and again: "Instead of monastic flight from the world the duty is now emphasized of serving God in the world, in every position in life." This was what I had felt for years, yet I was aware of few Christians who spoke like this. I was more familiar with an approach to Christian faith whose watchword was "beware of the world" and whose admonition was "don't love the world." This resistance to taking life "in the world" too seriously had an attractive spiritual veneer, especially when expressed by a passionate and eloquent preacher, missionary, or spiritual expert whom I would hear in church, at conference, or on Christian radio. The truth of the matter is that even though I was excited to have this new theological air to breathe, I was also hearing a passionate spiritual counterargument in my head. After reading Kuyper, it took a while to move beyond internal conversations like this:

Me: At last I see that I've been right for years about engaging the world.

Spiritual Voice (SV): Are you sure about that? The Bible tells us that we shouldn't love the world. Aren't your priorities out of order?

Me: I don't think so. Don't we have a role to play in society?

SV: Everything we do should be to the glory of God, and that means we show our allegiance to God by connecting everything to the gospel. How can you do that if you waste time with politics or strain to find something to appreciate in the secular world? Besides, you're in danger of getting corrupted by "bad company" if you get involved in the world. Remember what James 4:4 says: "Friendship with the world means enmity against God."

Me: Jesus is Lord of my life, and I want nothing more than to live fully for him. I think we can be faithful by getting involved in society in a way that pleases God. Isn't God pleased if we simply do things well, whether we are a politician, musician, or teacher?

SV: Is that connecting it to the gospel? If you really want to please God "out there," you have to find a way to make sure you are a witness. It has to be like Paul's desire to become all things to all people in order to introduce people to Jesus.

Me: What about expressing our faithfulness to God by trying to do our best in every area of life and even trying to change the world? Isn't it worthwhile to make life better for all of us?

SV: The Bible tells us the world will only get worse and worse. It's a waste of time trying to improve things. The ship is going down! Everything we do has to point toward being a good witness to the gospel. Maybe things will get a little better if more individuals get saved, but we can't afford to waste time on improving society. It's a loser's game. Only what you do for Christ will last, and those are eternal things like helping people know Jesus.

Me: I know what you mean, but I'm not sure. Something seems right about what Kuyper says. Let me think about it some more.

While imaginary conversations like this took place for quite a while, I eventually was able to see how God's work of common grace actually compels us toward the path of engaging the world without compromising our allegiance to Jesus.

"How do we find that path?" I had asked that question since college days; I have learned that others share the same deep concern. It is a legitimate concern, because many of us have heard stories about Christians who had an unfortunate shift of priorities precisely because they became enamored by their participation in politics, business, music, and so on. But the existence of cautionary tales is not a sufficient reason to disengage; the mere existence of bad examples does not automatically direct us to avoid seeking the right way to participate in the world.

So how do we get there? How exactly does common grace work, and what does it mean for the way we regard this world? How is this sound theology instead of wish fulfillment for a fan of culture and public life?

Common grace directs our attention to God's creation and also leads us to a big question: How do we understand what the Bible says when it talks about "the world"? Kuyper's quote assumes that we live in a fallen world, just like the Spiritual Voice in my imaginary conversations. Yet Christians differ in their perspective on the proper priorities for a faithful life in light of a fallen creation. The Spiritual Voice in my head would say that a fallen world means that we should live in a way that shows we resist unnecessary participation in society; cultural engagement and political concerns should not distract us from our chief priorities of evangelism and discipleship. We should live in a way that shows we are a part of God's distinctive people. But Kuyper and the doctrine of common grace lead us to think more broadly. God shows mercy to his creation by restraining the full effects of the fall, and this makes it possible for people to still glorify God by participating in every area of life.

Perhaps some of my confusion came from the fact that I saw the words *creation* and *world* as nearly identical. Any talk of engaging creation was the same as "living in the world" and displeasing God, since texts like 1 John 2:15 – 17 tell us not to love the world. In my mind, it was like saying that while Genesis 1:31 tells us that God calls the creation "very good," Genesis 3 introduces a new verdict: the creation is now the fallen world that belongs to the Evil One. If the creation were the same as the world, it would indeed be very much like the sinking ship voiced by my imagination (and many other real voices in some traditions). In a sinking ship, the top priority is to get people off the boat and onto something like a salvation lifeboat that will eventually carry them away to the heavenly shore. A closer look at the Bible, however, revealed that I was confused.

The Greek word translated as "world" in the Bible has a range of meanings that includes "creation" but also includes "world system," or the way one lives in the creation. When I took a closer look at 1 John 2:15 – 17, I saw something that had escaped my notice when I memorized it in college: the way that the text describes "the world" as something we should not love does not refer directly to creation. We are told that the world we are to avoid is characterized by misdirected desires of our senses and sight and by self-boasting. "The world" is a matter of dispositions, not the creation itself. This was news to me, and I came to understand that loving the world refers to a way of living in God's creation with an allegiance to someone other than the Creator. The person who loves the world is someone who lives in the created order in a way that disregards the instructions for us given by the Designer.

The First Great Commission

This clarified perspective helped me see that the important issue is how we go about living in God's creation as opposed to finding ways of escaping from it. Going back to the beginning of the Bible, I saw that we had been given a job from the start. Genesis 1:26 and 28 had never really grabbed my attention before, but this text emphasizes that humans have dignity because they were made in the image of God. The part about having dominion over creation never seemed all that important to me; perhaps I thought it was mostly about agriculture. But my encounter with Kuyper helped me understand that there was more than one Great Commission in the Bible. While Matthew 28:19–20 commands us to make disciples of the nations, Genesis 1:26 and 28 reveal that humans were commanded to cultivate the creation, to lead it to flourishing as the result of the best kind of stewardship. Human beings were created in God's image, and an essential part of demonstrating this divine image is working with the creation in a way that displays the best sense of "rule."* Without question, Genesis 3 throws a wrench into this original Great Commission, but we would be mistaken if we thought that fallenness absolves us of any further responsibility apart from providing an exit strategy from the created order.

Common grace makes it possible for us to continue to

---

* As I will mention later, it is important to note that many have interpreted "dominion" in a way that gives sanction to ravaging or neglecting the created order, and in some cases this language has been associated with some of the worst expressions of political conquest. This is why understanding "dominion," or "rule," as steward-like care is essential. We can think of it this way: we would only regard a ruler positively if they lead their kingdom to flourishing, if they are good stewards of the domain under their care.

obey the first Great Commission. The reality of the fall means that our task will be much harder than it was at the beginning because many people participate in the creation in ways that are distorted. It is often considered normal for life in God's creation to reflect the worldliness we see in 1 John 2:15 – 17. In spite of the challenges we face due to the fall, common grace encourages us to remember that God has never said, "You remember that first commandment? Forget it. It's meaningless now." Common grace is a doctrine that gives us a vision for seeing one vital part of Christian faithfulness. While it is vitally important to proclaim the gospel, introduce people to Jesus, and help them move toward faithful discipleship as they participate in church life, it is also tremendously important for Christians to see that it has always been our responsibility to care for the world, cultivating the flourishing of life through our activity in culture, politics, education, medicine, business, and every public area. One way to think of it is to say that the initial command given to humans can only be most fully displayed by those who are on the way to becoming more fully human. This is true of Christians because they are followers of Jesus (he was the ultimate human as well as fully divine). Common grace helps us recognize that faithful life in God's world means the pursuit of bringing God glory by demonstrating how the various aspects of society can work properly. There is another important benefit: in light of the fact that most Christians aren't involved in jobs that are directly connected to the mission of the church, common grace helps us all see why the work we do has significance. Life beyond Sunday has meaning.

One other benefit is that common grace leads us to take God's creation seriously instead of seeing it as ultimately evil. Many Christians with the best of intentions end up sounding like the ancient heretics called Gnostics who thought that the material world was evil. I have heard Christians talk about the gospel as the great escape from this creation with an eagerness that at times sounds like they have forgotten that the incarnation of Christ means that the material world is ultimately good and will be redeemed (Romans 8:19 – 22). While there are many reasons to grieve the ills we see all around the world, and days when the refrain "Come quickly, Lord Jesus" seems to be the only appropriate response, our responsibility for the life of the creation does not ultimately allow us to say, "This world is not my home; I'm just passing through." While understanding that many people make such statements to express their allegiance to God and their detachment from the materialistic cultural and political idolatries that surround us, I fear that such thoughts become a spiritual escape clause that gives permission to abdicate our role in creation. Even for those who disagree, the question is, what will they do with their life while they are here? How will they live a life that glorifies God not only in the church but also in the other areas of life? If they are unable to connect other parts of their life to evangelism, how do they have significance?

What are we to make of all the time spent in public, particularly when it is spent on efforts that contribute to building and maintaining society? Indeed, most of us will not be in full-time Christian service as a vocation, and the majority of our week will not be spent on things with the label "spiritual." For most of us, then, how does most of life beyond Sunday matter? I believe common grace helps us answer this question.

From a different angle, another question arises: What if a person lives in a place that restricts participation in public life? Does this change how we understand our life in creation or even give good reason for looking for an exit strategy instead of terms of engagement? I don't think it does. The difficulty that emerges as a result of Genesis 3 is certainly on display in many countries where there is little if any opportunity to contribute to the public aspects of life in ways that bring God glory. Life in a setting like Malaysia or North Korea significantly narrows the options for public obedience to the first Great Commission, yet our responsibility remains. In circumstances like these, Christians truly find themselves in exilic settings where they must pray for and look for opportunities for creation stewardship that give what may only amount to a faint aroma or brief glimpse of forms of social, cultural, and political life that glorify God. In these circumstances, our faithfulness to our responsibility for the creation will often take a form of what some call "alternative witness." The expressions of cultural engagement and sociopolitical development may take place more within the confines of the Christian community than within the public realm, but this does not mean that Christians in exilic contexts stop looking for opportunities to penetrate and transform the culture. The Christian community is a place to model and practice our stewardship wherever we are, and when the public opportunity arrives, we should pursue it with both wisdom and vigor.

Another question that sometimes emerges at the mention of "creation stewardship" is whether the dominion given to humans is license for wreaking havoc on the earth in selfish and careless ways. It is certainly true that some Christians have disregarded our responsibility for God's world either because of an overemphasis on "spiritual" over "material" things or because they actually believe *dominion* is a code word for ruthless domination of the earth. These mistaken emphases should not cause us to shrink from our responsibility. Rather, we should remember that to be a steward of God's earth implies that we are responsible to God for faithfully attending to the task given to us. If we understand that we are "responsible" stewards, we can never participate in the created order in a careless way. Instead, we will be the standard bearers for the care of creation that is expressed environmentally, politically, educationally, culturally, and so on.

A great opportunity has always been there for us. God in mercy has made it possible for us to participate in others' lives with a greater degree of fullness than many of us can imagine. Every area of life is terrain for bringing God glory. Many of us need "permission" to enter this terrain while others need to be made aware that it is part of our map. Now we know what is there for us. The public domain is there for our participation and transformative presence.

2

PERSPECTIVE:
IDENTITY AND ALLEGIANCE

THE 1972 PRESIDENTIAL ELECTION IS ONE OF MY EARLIEST memories about politics. I remember that in our house the crystal-clear candidate of choice was George McGovern. Though much else remains fuzzy, I recall that the reasons for voting for McGovern were mostly related to party affiliation. In the Bacote household it was natural to vote for the Democratic candidate because that was the party that was "for us" — *us* referring to African Americans. At that time Democrats were the party associated with supporting policies intended to remedy the history of racial discrimination in the United States.

As a seven-year-old, I was unaware of the shift in the 1960s when some Democrats became less known as Dixiecrats and Republicans became less known as the party of Lincoln. All I knew was that my parents were not going to vote for Nixon, and when 1976 came around they were definitely voting for Carter.

I did not arrive at these assumptions because of passionate political argument in our home or because of the influence of media on my relatively innocent mind; it occurred simply because I was there. Like breathing the unseen air, the flow of many conversations among my parents and extended family created an ethos where I came to regard support of the Democratic Party as natural, and at some unarticulated level I assumed that this was the stance of true justice. No one demanded that I have that view of things, but I was unable to imagine any other kind of political loyalty.

There's another way to view this: my self-understanding was that I was a member of a family in the state of Maryland, and I was a citizen of the United States. I grew up Baptist, and though I am sure I believed the truth of the gospel by age eight or nine, I didn't join the church and get baptized until after age eleven. My understanding of my faith at that time was that Christians have eternal life because of Jesus and that we should be obedient to God. It was a very personal faith. I had a strong desire to be a good Christian, and I knew that God should be my first loyalty above all others. But this loyalty to God had no explicit connection to my "natural" loyalty to the Democratic Party. Back then, if someone had asked me whether Jesus cares about public life, I would not have had any kind of clear answer besides a noncommittal "I guess so," though I did assume that good Christians would always vote for the Democratic Party because justice was on our side.*

Looking back during those years, I find it interesting that while I was arriving at the assumption that Democrats were on the side of justice, some evangelical Christians were becoming politically vocal regarding abortion rights (the *Roe v. Wade* decision occurred in 1973, when I was eight) and 1976 was

---

* Truth be told, this was essentially single-issue politics, or perhaps more precisely, a form of identity politics that extended to multiple political concerns. To my mind then, it was one issue: the support and survival of African Americans.

"The Year of the Evangelical" according to *Time* and *Newsweek*. Though I knew the United States was at odds with the Soviet Union (I didn't learn the term *Cold War* until high school), I did not know that *communism* was code for "hostility to Christianity" in the eyes of many believers. I also had little idea that evangelical Protestants were revving up for a return to political engagement after several decades of absence, and I was certainly unaware that a majority of evangelicals would identify with the Republican party by the time Jimmy Carter was swept out of the White House by Ronald Reagan. But I did know I was a Christian who lived in the United States, with separate loyalties to Jesus and a political party. I belonged to someone (God) and had a political allegiance to my country in general and one party in particular.

Uncertainty and Change

When I went off to college, the relationship I perceived between Christian faith and public life began to become clearer, though also more complicated. I had an experience common among many African Americans who come from Bible-believing churches: I joined a Bible study with other Christians who shared a similar commitment to Jesus but a different political allegiance. Though I did not recognize it at the time, this was my formal entry into the evangelical subculture. The political dissonance did not cause a great crisis in my friendships because I did not reveal my shock at learning that there were Bible-believing Christians who were Republicans. I cherished this Bible study group and kept my political commitments close to my chest while silently wondering how they (and the majority of people at the church I attended) could "naturally" assume that the Republican Party deserved our support in the 1984 presidential election. I rarely broached political topics with my circle of Christian friends; besides, as the previous chapter reveals, the bigger issue was the spiritual conflict raised by my love of rock music. Yet a slow change was happening.

By the time I graduated from college, I had a much greater familiarity with the evangelical subculture and had immense gratitude for the spiritual formation I received though my Bible study, Christian friendships, and church. Soon after graduation, I decided that one of the ways to make sure I kept growing in my faith was to have a steady diet of Christian radio. Though it may seem incredibly naïve to say this, I granted considerable authority to the preachers and talk-show hosts I heard each day. My assumption was that if they were on an evangelical radio station, then they were presenting a perspective that flowed from the Bible. Even if there was some disagreement on certain issues, there was enough continuity in the larger frame, and I granted trust to the voices I heard. While I mostly listened to preachers such as Chuck Swindoll, Charles Stanley, and John MacArthur, I also listened to issues-oriented programs that addressed topics related to family life, politics, and culture. Of course James Dobson's *Focus on the Family* and D. James Kennedy's *Truths That Transform* were prominent in this regard.

Given the trust granted to voices I heard in my car and sometimes at work, I began to develop a view of how Christians should think about life in the United States and broader world. The pro-life cause (particularly advocacy for laws that restricted abortion) and the resistance to political policies that would yield advantage to the Eastern European communist regimes featured prominently, along with various forms of commentary related to the restoration of the United States to its Judeo-Christian heritage. When it came to national elections for the president and Congress, a significant change occurred: I came to the position that fidelity to Christ meant voting for Republican candidates because they were the pro-life and more pro-American political party.

One might ask at this juncture, "What about that allegiance to the Democratic Party because of their commitment to the concerns of African Americans?" I still had concerns about the issues of education, employment, and genuine access to pathways toward the American Dream, but I was convinced that many positive advances had occurred as a result of the Civil Rights movement and was not convinced that some forms of welfare and affirmative action were as helpful as originally intended. The greater reason for the shift ultimately lay in a matter of both identity and allegiance. I wanted my identity to emerge from commitment to Christ as Lord over the entirety of my life, and it seemed that one of the best ways to embody that loyalty was through a commitment to the political issues that were given great emphasis in the evangelical subculture. Race remained a tremendously important concern, but my awareness of issues like abortion and the biblically based argument made for the pro-life position led me to a conviction that I could only vote for pro-life candidates, which tended to mean Republican candidates for national offices.* I wished for a

---

* The argument was ultimately a human dignity argument rooted in the biblical view of humans as created in the image of God and in the prohibition against murder. The unborn child in the womb from conception is a person, not merely a disposable clump of cells. Of course, this argument was not only a matter of biblical exegesis but was also informed by philosophy and by a natural-law argument in some cases.

political reality where the concerns about race as well as abortion were equally addressed by the same candidate, but this remained a dream. The centerpiece for me was the intersection of my identity as a Christian and the ultimate loyalties that I hoped would spring from fidelity to the lordship of Christ. With a more explicit relationship between my faith and public concerns, I was hopeful that I could have a faith characterized by public and private faithfulness.

While my desire was (and remains) simple in verbal expression, it is more complex in actual practice, as exemplified by the reality that faithful Christians support candidates across the political spectrum. Christians in my family and even some of my close Christian friends in evangelical circles arrived at different political conclusions, though they also had a desire to have Christ on the throne of their lives. In the years since the late 1980s, though evangelicals have still tended to favor Republican candidates, there has been greater attention given to those who identify as evangelical while supporting candidates who are Democratic or Libertarian, and even some who try to have great distance between themselves and explicit political commitments. This diverse state of affairs presents us with a significant dilemma: How do Christians regard themselves and discern their loyalties to the different levels of human community? We are individuals who come from families, who live in neighborhoods located in certain countries in certain parts of the world, and whose lives belong to God.

Trying on Biblical Labels

What follows is an experiment to help discern our identity and allegiance. Without even the pretense of comprehensiveness, what happens if we take a number of prominent phrases or descriptions of identity from the biblical narrative and consider how they inform our self-perception? Following this, the experiment will conclude with the consideration of how to regard our identity and allegiance through the lens of "biblical" identity. While numerous books have been written on phrases that follow, and while many streams of tradition give emphasis to some labels more than others, the aim here is simply to consider some dimensions of these phrases as they inform the question of identity and have implications for our loyalties.

"Image of God"

This phrase takes us to the beginning of the biblical narrative and our creation as human beings. One of the most important dimensions of the *image of God* language in Genesis is that all humans are considered bearers of the divine image, which was a stark contrast with other perspectives in the Ancient Near East that only regarded kings or males as some reflection of a deity. Genesis 1:27 directly states that both male and female are created in the image of the creator, and this "royal dignity" is reaffirmed in texts such as Genesis 9:6 and Psalm 8. The biblical view of humans as divine image bearers establishes our identity as the unique pinnacle of God's creation order and as those whose common status serves as a basis for mutual respect. This is implicit in the prohibition against murder in Genesis 9:6 as well as in the wondrous poetic language in Psalm 8. Our common humanity *ought* to be in view when we think about the regard due to each person. A second important element of humans as divine image bearers is that they are given the task of being servant-rulers who have the task of stewarding God's creation.[4] This first commission given to humans implies that human identity best operates when it is oriented toward leading the world to its flourishing. To be human is to have fidelity to God expressed as respect for others and concern for cultivating a world that honors the One who created it. The language of humans as divine image bearers does not immediately suggest greater or lesser fidelity to our immediate geographic location, nor does it give us explicit rules that would give detailed framing to public policy, but it does suggest that our loyalty to God may imply commitments to humans that extend beyond local communal identities.

"Children of Abraham"

We encounter this phrase further into the biblical narrative, though it is unlikely to be one of the first labels Christians will use to describe themselves. The Bible gives no explanation regarding why God called out to Abram. Genesis 12 begins by telling us that God called out Abram from his clan, commanded him to begin the journey to an undisclosed land, and made the great promise that he would be the father of a great nation, a recipient of divine blessing, and ultimately one whose legacy would culminate in blessing the entire earth. Abram is eventually renamed Abraham and becomes the patriarch of the nation of Israel, God's chosen people.

One interesting dimension to consider is that most Christians today have a Gentile heritage. Though we see the apostles overcome their resistance to the inclusion of the Gentiles in Acts 10 – 15, we get a clearer sense of Gentile Christians as recipients of Abraham's legacy through Paul's words in texts like Galatians 3:6 – 29. There Paul strongly argues that all who believe in Christ are children of Abraham and heirs because of the fulfillment of God's promise to bless all nations. *Children of Abraham* conveys that God's people have an identity that includes being both the chosen recipients of God's promise to bring the blessing of salvation to the world and a corporate, communal identity that is shared with others from across ethnic and national identities as the result of the fulfillment of the promise. If the children of Abraham can be found across the globe, how do we begin to think of who "we" are, especially when, as heirs of Abraham's promise, we share an ultimate commonality that culminates in the life together with God in the new heavens and earth?

"People of the Covenant"

This label is related to the Abrahamic legacy. While one could argue that covenants with God are present as early as Genesis 2, the specific covenant in mind here is the covenant God made with Israel, the covenant that was renewed in Joshua 24 where we find phrases that sometimes appear on the walls of Christian homes:

> Then choose for yourselves this day whom you will serve, ... But as for me and my household, we will serve the LORD. (v. 15)

> We will serve the LORD our God and obey him. (v. 24)

These pledges of fidelity to God meant that the Israelites intended to honor their covenantal agreement with God. Covenantal agreements contain both promises tied to fidelity and consequences for infidelity. By agreeing to be God's covenant people, they were making a kind of marriage vow with him, pledging fidelity and loyalty to the end. Of course, the Old Testament narrative contains enough peaks and valleys to satisfy the greatest roller-coaster enthusiast, and ultimately Israel's covenantal infidelity results in exile. Yet even when God gives many warnings of the exile to come, as we see in the prophets, he promises to maintain fidelity to his part of the covenant promises.

If Christians regard themselves as God's covenant people as part of their Abrahamic heritage brought to fruition in Christ, the covenant relationship not only informs our identity but clearly makes claims on our ultimate loyalties. Though we are in the era of grace and not law, the covenantal dimension reveals that we are people who truly belong to God and are united by God. Our reception of grace is central to our access and reception of this covenant relationship, but the grace of salvation apart from works does not diminish the claim that our covenant relationship makes on our identity. If we reckon with this claim, then we must continually ask ourselves how a label like *people of the covenant* informs the way we determine and prioritize our sense of obligation and fidelity.

"Follower of Jesus"

This takes us into the New Testament and might be the trickiest of all the labels in our experiment. Variants of this phrase have become a popular way for a large number of people to identify with Jesus while creating distance from negative associations with the word *Christian*. Whether the bad press is deserved or not, the label *Christian* currently seems to have more liabilities attached than *follower of Jesus* or *Jesus follower*. Jesus is more popular than Christians. The reason the label is tricky, however, stems from a fundamental question: What version of Jesus are people choosing to follow? Is it a peace-loving Jesus who would never hurt a fly and only talked about a love that makes no demands on anyone? Is it a Jesus who taught great moral truths? Is it a Jesus who was a political leader who embodied nonviolent resistance to a world intoxicated by power and coercion? Or is it perhaps a Jesus who was merely human and an inspiring figure but not the Savior of the world? The list could go on and on.

For this label to have integrity, it requires us to resist a consumer-oriented, buffet-style approach to the biblical revelation about Jesus. The central reason *follower of Jesus* is a label stems from the fact that his words were sometimes an invitation (for example, Mark 1:17) and other times a command (Mark 2:14, John 21:22): "Follow me." We also find texts such as 1 Peter 2:21 that draw on events from Christ's ministry (in this case his suffering) as a model for us to follow in certain circumstances. If we trace the narrative of the gospel with an eye toward what it means to follow Jesus, what becomes clear is that those who chose to follow Jesus experienced him not only as a unique and superior teacher but also as one who required the ultimate allegiance of his followers. This allegiance meant not only intellectually embracing his teaching but also living a life that revealed their commitment to him, even to the point of death (see Mark 8:34 – 9:1). While I write this in a country where the likelihood of facing death as a result of fidelity to Christ is very low, the cost of following Jesus remains, and the call for commitment is no less intense. If *follower of Jesus* is a label that is taken seriously at full intensity, it is actually not as tricky a matter as it first seems when we think about our loyalties.

Followers of Jesus are people whose allegiance to their Messiah is a first priority in any context.

"Aliens and Pilgrims"

First Peter 1:1 and 2:11 give us language about Christian identity that highlights distinctiveness. *Strangers*, *aliens*, and *exiles* are the terms that appear in various English translations of 1:1 to indicate the outsider status of Peter's audience, Jewish and Gentile Christians who were living in cities away from Israel and experiencing persecution. In 2:11 *pilgrims* or *sojourners* (depending upon the translation) appear along with the term from 1:1 and broadens this identity to include an emphasis on the journey of Christians toward the consummation of salvation. This type of identity is one of the key sources for phrases like "This world is not my home, I'm just passing through," and leads us to consider how a vocabulary of "otherness" factors into our overall self-perception as Christians. To be a stranger, alien, sojourner, or pilgrim means that our sense of belonging to God will exist with some level of tension with our immediate home. Though it is fair to ask whether the label is only relevant in circumstances analogous to that in 1 Peter, the abundant language of distinctiveness throughout the New Testament strongly suggests that to be Christian is to be some kind of "other" even in seemingly friendly contexts. One major question that arises is whether this identity of "otherness" compels us to keep our distance from involvement in the structures of society when such participation is possible. As I argued in chapter one, I do not believe this to be the case. Still, any label suggestive of foreignness indicates that when we consider the question of allegiance, we might always have to put an asterisk next to any loyalties besides God and his kingdom.

"The Church"

One could argue that much of what I have written thus far is nothing more than defining what it means to be the church, but there is one dimension of this specific label worth highlighting as part of our experiment. Long ago I went to my concordance to survey every use of the word "church" in the New Testament and discovered that the dominant meaning of the term referred to a gathering of people analogous to the way we might think of "community" or simply "group of people." Though a word study alone is not sufficient to unpack the full meaning of *church*, it certainly gives us one vital window into the concept. To be the *church* is to be part of a group of people united under God, a community whose identity stems from the One who has brought them together and given them a purpose.

While no one would ever accuse me of being an Anabaptist, there is truth to the sense that the church is a community that exists as an alternate corporate entity that models a set of commitments and practices distinct from other communities. While Christians may disagree about which commitments and practices make the church distinct, there is no question that the church should be, as expressed in the King James Version of 1 Peter 2:9, a "peculiar" people. If the church is to witness to such peculiarity, what types of public actions tell the world what "church" looks like?

"Citizens"

Ephesians 2:19 and Philippians 3:20 employ the language of citizenship to highlight two important aspects of Christian identity. In Ephesians Paul is telling his audience of Gentile

Christians that they now belong to the people of God, and *citizens* conveys the truth of all the rights and privileges that go along with this new peoplehood. There are no special or hidden clauses in some secret document that say the Gentiles have limited privileges; they have the entire package, and Paul also uses the language of "household" to make this point clear. In Philippians, Paul says "our citizenship is in heaven" as a mark of belonging and identity as he encourages his audience to follow godly examples. While the Philippians may have taken pride in being citizens of Rome, Paul's language provides a strong contrast that calls for the ultimate loyalty to God and his people. A slogan like "Jesus is Lord and not Caesar" lies behind this allegiance and the call for a lifestyle reflective of the true King. *Christian* equals *citizen* of God's kingdom.

Though hardly exhaustive of Christian identity, the cumulative effect of these seven phrases alone show us that to be a human being and to be one who belongs to God implies a sense of identity and allegiance that goes far beyond what any of us would likely say if someone asked, "Who are you?" and "Where are your loyalties?" If phrases like "putting God first" are to be weightier than if they were uttered by a myna bird, then we must reckon with the obligations that come with privileges of being divine image bearers united to God through Christ.

Our Place

It would be simplistic as well as misguided to suggest that our belonging to God leads us away from reckoning with another indisputable fact: we all live somewhere. We cannot wrestle with the question of identity and allegiance if we practice a spiritual escapism that masquerades as loyalty to God's kingdom. Each of us currently has some kind of address in a city that is part of some region of some nation somewhere on this globe. Though technology has made many advances and *virtual reality* is part of our accepted vocabulary, we all still have a land-based connection. My driver's license is issued by a particular state, and I vote for candidates in elections held in my state and nation. When national holidays come around, I see many people waving the Stars and Stripes at parades, and if the military is represented, it is only soldiers serving in the armed forces of the United States that anyone expects to see. These facts cannot be simply pushed aside. We are citizens of towns and nations, and our daily conduct often reveals that we take this truth for granted.*

Though God demands top priority, this does not entail a commitment to treason in our lands of citizenship. Among the places where Scripture gives us guidance in this matter, I will highlight two types of commands that can help us put our loyalties in perspective. The first example comes from Jeremiah 29:7, part of a letter the prophet sent from Jerusalem to all the people of Judah after Nebuchadnezzar, king of Babylon, conquered them and took them into exile. Though the exile came because God punished the people for great covenantal infidelity, they were still given words of comfort and direction. The directive in verse 7 is remarkable. After telling the exiles to settle down, God then tells them to "seek the peace and prosperity of the city to which I have carried you into exile. Pray to the LORD for it, because if it prospers, you too will prosper."

---

* Of course, I say this aware of the fact that immigration is a significant issue in many parts of the world. The main point is that we are all citizens of some country, even if we might desire citizenship elsewhere.

While we might think that God would be instructing them to pray for the vanquishing of Babylon and a return to Jerusalem, God instead tells them to pray that the land of their exile will flourish.

What might this mean for Christians today? Though the exile of Israel and Judah occurs in a far different context than what many Christians experience today, the command to pray for the prosperity of the lands in which we find ourselves remains important. This command also puts before us the question of what should come to our mind when we consider Christians who are in other countries, particularly those that are hostile or indifferent to the faith. As a Christian in the United States, I often wonder what opinion American evangelical Christians have about the disposition and perspective of our fellow Christians in other countries. What perspective should they have? Do we expect them to pray for the best for their country? Does it even cross our minds, aside from hoping for the gospel to advance in the lives of individuals beyond our borders? This command suggests that regardless of our location, we should pray for nations to flourish because such flourishing may likely be beneficial for all who dwell in that land.

First Timothy 2:1 – 2 emphasizes a similar idea, though Paul states it less as a command than a plea. He instructs Timothy to teach others to pray for all people and then especially focuses on governmental authorities. Ultimately, this is another prayer for peace so that Christians find themselves in settings where they can live faithful Christian lives without duress. It is notable that Paul does not say to pray only for good governmental officials or for those whose policies resonate with our own commitments. In many places around the world, political discourse thrives on attacking the opposition, and the warlike dimensions of politics can often work against the greater good of a country or smaller locale. A notable implication from both this text and Jeremiah 29:7 may be that Christians exhibit a distinctive practice of praying for the good of leaders and nations even when it may seem counterintuitive. How many of us pray for the good of leaders in North Korea or Iran or nations known for corruption?

The second type of command is found in both Romans 13:1 – 7 and 1 Peter 2:12 – 14. The core imperative in both sets of verses is that Christians are to be good citizens who live exemplary lives in submission to the government in light of the fact that God has provided rulers to punish evil and commend the good. Neither Paul nor Peter were writing to people in settings where the rulers were God-fearing people, yet they urge believers to be people who are on the right side of the law and upstanding citizens. One of the most important implications here is that our identity as citizens in cities, states, and nations is to be taken seriously. Though Christians have a greater allegiance to God than to any earthly nation or political figure, it is proper Christian practice to be a good citizen.

As I write this, I can hear the voices of those who say, "But isn't there a place for Christians to be revolutionaries in crisis situations that demand opposition to government oppression?" Two things come to mind here. First, in countries where Christians are able to participate at the various levels of government, as in some modern democratic societies, one of the main ways to participate and advocate for change is by involvement in the system, whether that is as simple as voting or as complicated as serving in public office. Second, in countries where such participation is either a farce or clearly not possible, the Christian community has an opportunity to model an approach to life that may be revolutionary without resorting to violent measures. The context will matter immensely in this regard, but we should at least begin with the commitment to be good citizens first before resorting to revolution.

Where does this bring us with the question of perspective? What guidance does a biblical and theological view of our identity as human beings give us as we go about our lives on this planet? I close with what may be more of a gesture than a prescription: Christians belong to God, and they also live all around the world in various places under a range of government systems. Even if we live in a country like the United States that, as G. K. Chesterton suggested, in some way has "the soul of a church," our loyalty to country can never be confused with our prime allegiance to the triune God with whom we are in covenant relationship. Moreover, even if the idea of American exceptionalism has some degree of truth, this hardly equates with the realization of God's kingdom on earth and my fidelity to God cannot be easily equated with a patriotism that diminishes the view of fellow Christians elsewhere.* Rather, whether we are in cities and nations that are supportive or hostile, we have a constant challenge to see ourselves first as kingdom citizens who are committed to the good of all nations, whether this is limited to praying for justice or the active and patient construction of better societies. Of course we care about life within our borders, but we also share a world with other divine image-bearers.

---

* By "American exceptionalism" I mean the belief, implicit or otherwise, that the United States of America is unlike other nations and that its uniqueness makes it in some way a superior country in God's plan. For some Christians, this includes the idea of the United States as a nation chosen by God.

3

POSTURE:
PURSUING PUBLIC HOLINESS

THOUGH I WOULD NOT REGARD MYSELF AS AN AFICIONADO of the vampire genre, I enjoyed the film adaptation of *Interview with the Vampire: The Vampire Chronicles* in 1994. Anne Rice became famous as the author of this series of novels and was known for having dedicated followers. Though she had grown up Roman Catholic, she became an atheist as a young adult and was hardly a likely candidate to write favorable stories about religion. Thus, it was a surprise to many when she made a public return to Catholicism in 1998 and eventually wrote two fictionalized (but not irreverent) novels about the life of Jesus. Her story took another surprise turn in 2010 when she made this post on her Facebook page: "For those who care, and I understand if you don't: Today I quit being a Christian. I'm out. I remain committed to Christ as always but not to being 'Christian' or being part of Christianity. It's simply impossible for me to 'belong' to this quarrelsome, hostile, disputatious, and deservedly infamous group. For ten years, I've tried. I've failed. I'm an outsider. My conscience will allow nothing else."

In a subsequent interview with *Christianity Today* she said,

> I wanted my readers to know that I was stepping aside from organized religion and the names *Christian* and *Christianity* because I wanted to exonerate myself from the things organized religion was doing in the name of Jesus. Christians have lost credibility in America as people who know how to love. They have become associated with hatred, persecution, attempting to abolish the separation of church and state, and trying to pressure people to vote certain ways in elections. I wanted to make it clear that I did not in any way remain complicit with those things. I never expected anyone beyond my Facebook page would be interested. I was doing this for my readers to let them know.[5]

Rice's defection was less about Jesus than about a set of associations with the labels *Christ* and *Christianity* that struck her as mean-spirited and hateful. She is not alone.

In May 2012 one of my students sent me a link to a blog post by Rachel Held Evans with the title "How to Win a Culture War and Lose a Generation." While the catalyst for the article was the election that included Amendment One in North Carolina (which made it unconstitutional for the state to recognize or perform same sex marriages or civil unions), this specific issue was a flashpoint and symbol for a larger concern. In language similar to Rice, Evans expressed a sentiment felt by her and many of her readers:

> We are tired of fighting, tired of vain efforts to advance the Kingdom through politics and power, tired of drawing lines in the sand, tired of being known for what we are against, not what we are for....

So my question for those evangelicals leading the charge in the culture wars is this: *Is it worth it?*

Is a political "victory" really worth losing millions more young people to cynicism regarding the Church?

Is a political "victory" worth further alienating people who identify as LGBT?

Is a political "victory" worth perpetuating the idea that evangelical Christians are at war with gays and lesbians?

And is a political "victory" worth drowning out that quiet but persistent internal voice that asks — *what if we get this wrong?*

Too many Christian leaders seem to think the answer to that question is "yes," and it's costing them.[6]

The members of the generation referred to by Evans are younger Christians, mostly millennials, though without question these same frustrations have been expressed by Christians beyond the age of thirty-five. Like Rice, Evans expresses the concerns that the public commitments and actions of Christians are antagonistic and unloving rather than Christlike. "Where is the love?" seems to be a question that hangs in the air.

In Evans's post, she makes reference to David Kinnaman and Gabe Lyons' *unChristian: What a New Generation Really Thinks about Christianity ... and Why It Matters* (2007). Though at least seven years have passed since the book's publication, the public image of Christianity reported within remains. The approach of the book was to ask those outside Christianity to share their perception of Christians, and the now-familiar list of unfavorable images included labels such as anti-homosexual (91%), judgmental (87%), hypocritical (85%), too involved in politics (75%), and insensitive to others (70%).[7] There were positive labels as well, but it is the negative perceptions that are troubling. There is clearly an image problem linked to the idea that Christians are essentially "haters" who want to make society safe for their kind of people and harsh for those who disagree.

Dan Merchant's 2010 documentary entitled *Lord, Save Us from Your Followers* also investigates this image problem. The film asks us to consider how it could be that a gospel of love is a source of division in a country where most people profess belief in God. Merchant went across the country and did a series of interviews with people (including well-known figures) from a wide range of beliefs and found that public discussion of faith does not need to be contentious. We invited him to our campus for a screening of the film, and during the question time he was asked, "But isn't the gospel supposed to be offensive?" In response he stated his agreement that the gospel can be offensive but then noted that his great concern was that Christians could be so personally offensive that an encounter with the gospel never occurs. The theme is familiar.

Anne Rice, Rachel Held Evans, Dave Kinnaman, Gabe Lyons, and Dan Merchant are only a few of the people expressing concern about the public image and public practice of Christians. As a professor at a Christian College I have encountered this vexation many times. When my student sent me Evans's blog post, I asked him to help me understand his frustration in a subsequent email, and in part he said:

> I think my frustration lies primarily in the militant and arcane political approach of evangelicals.... I'm deeply disappointed that many evangelicals do not have a very substantive political ideology that mirrors the depth and complexity of the faith we subscribe to. The unfortunate

simplicity of our political voice is precisely why our ministry is negatively construed as nothing but "anti-homosexual."... I don't mean to undermine the magnitude of social issues, but to ask how could we not ascribe the same degree of passion toward other issues?

The bent of many Christian institutions that I've been a part of is to remain entrenched in traditions that appease the older, white, less-cultured majority. All other forms of competence that would be useful to Christians in a diverse world like ours are largely dismissed and deemed inapplicable to the personal development and sanctification of the believer. In its place, Christians are busy lobbying for anti-gay legislation, building conservative Christian universities, homeschooling their children, erecting massive megachurches, and moving farther and farther away from city centers where culture, in its brilliant complexity, is evolving by the minute. It feels as though evangelicals are forging their own proverbial plateau upon which they will sit above all the perversion and vulgarity of a society that they believe has lost sight of its Christian heritage (which is a debatable piece of our nation's history).

While my student expressed a number of concerns, the common thread for him and many others is a lingering frustration stemming from a public face of Christianity (particularly in its conservative, politically engaged expressions) manifested as the strong commitment to correct beliefs along with a strident, adversarial, and judgmental public posture. In conversations with students, I have directly encountered their vexation related to this problem. There is often confusion about what it means to be committed to truthfulness while also exhibiting care for others.

It reminds me of the time I was at a small event where musician Derek Webb performed. He had just put out his album *Stockholm Syndrome*, which was controversial in some circles because of the song "What Matters More." That song included a curse word and set the issue of homosexuality in the context of "50,000 people dyin' today." In a group conversation, Webb pointed out that he wrote songs like "What Matters More" because he knew many people with same-sex orientation who had experienced great mistreatment and abuse at the hands of Christians. The song asks whether some Christians' laser-like focus on the issue of homosexuality hasn't led to a corresponding myopic vision that misses or ignores other, possibly greater problems like world hunger. Many are still asking some version of this question. Since at least 2002, there have been reports that Christians want a holistic faith rooted in biblical truth but also rooted in public concerns other than homosexuality and abortion. Yet vexation seems to remain all around us; what does it look like to care about the truth and care about people at the same time?

Though these examples from Rice, Evans, Kinnaman/Lyons, and Webb (and countless millennials) have raised questions about the treatment of homosexual individuals, and while it would be true that for some of them their attention to the issue includes a form of advocacy, it would be a great mistake to think that a single issue is the ultimate or unique focus of the concern about the public posture of Christians. Though vexation about "culture wars" is one way to present these concerns, ultimately the central question is one about what it means to live out a public Christlikeness that exhibits equal care for people as well as issues.

Pursuing an Atypical Question

While one could certainly offer rebuttals regarding the accuracy of the negative public image above, the fact remains that a large number of people regard Christians negatively. Though there is a place for articulating our critiques of the image problem, I want to take another path and pose important questions to consider if we are to take public responsibility seriously as Christians: What does it mean to pursue holiness in a way that extends to and permeates the public dimension of our faith? What public posture emerges from taking holiness seriously? Though we may often think of holiness in terms of our internal personal piety (and indeed we should), the pursuit and expression of holiness is hardly antithetical to Christian engagement in public concerns such as politics.

For many years in my own journey of faith, holiness was immediately associated with certain dress codes (no pants or makeup for women, nothing flashy for men). The people I regarded as "holiness types" were those who had a narrow and restrictive faith, which had no place for my inclinations toward a culture-affirming version of Christian faith. Holiness people were like those who came from a foreign country, and the pursuit of holiness was primarily characterized by what one needed to avoid. Unsurprisingly, in my exposure to Christian public engagement (political or otherwise), holiness was rarely, if ever, part of the conversation about the public agenda of Christians (even in the cases where specific moral questions are at issue in public policy).

I see things much differently now. While there are good reasons to associate "holiness" or "sanctification" with codes of behavior characterized by things to be avoided, a closer look reveals that the distinctiveness of Christian life can be understood and expressed positively. By positive expression, I am not suggesting that Christians develop strategies to talk about holiness at town hall meetings or in letters to Congress; positive expression could perhaps include explicit conversation among fellow Christians, but beyond that, I am suggesting a broader approach to our rhetoric and practice in the broad domain of public responsibility.

To make our way to this broad approach to holiness, we must give attention to an area of subtle neglect. Many of us have a deficient Trinitarian theology. Though we may confess a belief in God the Father, God the Son, and God the Holy Spirit, the third member of the Trinity is often relegated to third place. In fifteen years of teaching, I have discovered that many students and church members have a common deficit: when asked what their churches taught them about the Holy Spirit, most have very little to say. A number of individuals' backgrounds could easily have contributed to this void, from those whose spiritual formation was in communities skeptical of Pentecostals and charismatics to those who simply were raised to be Christ-centered in a way that ultimately eclipsed the work of the Spirit. In either case, the result is often an approach to the Christian life that may be passionate but strangely (and at times intentionally) neglectful of God the Holy Spirit.

Some Christians might rightly suggest that the Holy Spirit is the subordinate member of the Trinity, deflecting attention from himself because of Jesus' statement about him in John 16:13 that "he will not speak on his own; he will speak only what he hears" and in the following verse: "He will glorify me because it is from me that he will receive what he will make known to you." Taken alone, there might be good reason to view the Holy Spirit as being primarily in the business of pointing to Jesus and operating in a manner similar to one who whispers to us while remaining hidden. If this were case, then scant attention to the Spirit would be proper Christian practice. Yet if we take the larger context into consideration, particularly Jesus's explanation in verse 15 that both the Son and Spirit are in continuity with the message and mission from God the Father, then it becomes clear that rather than telling us that the Spirit is subordinate, Jesus is telling us that the Holy Spirit is continuing God's work in the world after Christ departs. This truly makes him the Holy Comforter who comes alongside us after the ascension because we are not left alone after Christ is no longer physically with us. The Holy Spirit who is with us requires our attention if we are to best participate and benefit from God's mission in this world.

Toward Holiness

Though I am tempted to set forth a full theology of the Holy Spirit at this point, the focus here is on the transforming work of the Holy Spirit within God's people, the process of sanctification. By using the word *process*, I am putting my cards on the table: when we speak of Christians as God's holy people, it means more than the great truth that we belong to him and are set apart as his own. First Corinthians 1:2 helps us see both dimensions. As many of us might imagine, if there had been reality television in the first century, the Corinthian church would have had at least one or two shows of their own because of their dysfunction. Yet when Paul gives his salutation at the beginning of this epistle, he refers to them as "those sanctified in Christ Jesus" and "called to be his holy people." Even the Corinthians get the label of "holy people." These people belong to God and are given the task of living up to their identity. It's similar to when a parent says, "Do you know your last name? Then start acting like it." Paul's words also apply to us.

To put it another way, while the "set apartness" of Christians is part of our identity, as we saw in the previous chapter, this distinctiveness also refers to what is happening in our lives. The process of sanctification is an ongoing work of the Holy Spirit in Christians that should lead to a public display that reveals our identity. Or to put it in language common to many Christians, sanctification is a process that increasingly leads to our Christlikeness. When Christians ask God to help them be more like Jesus — when they sing songs about showing Jesus to the world, when they are exasperated by their encounters with the brokenness of fellow believers and wonder aloud or online whether Christians are reflecting Jesus — they are all really asking for God to do the work of sanctification by the Holy Spirit. All of the concern about how Christians operate in public is ultimately a question of whether there is evidence that the Holy Spirit is at work; is the disposition and discourse in any way indicative that Christ is being formed in people? If Christ is being formed in God's people by the Holy Spirit, has his work penetrated to those regions of the heart that reveal themselves in the domain of public responsibility?

It is interesting to observe that many of the complaints and reports of disappointment with Christians are often accompanied by the wish that there was more evidence of humanity in Christian public practice. Whether the concern is about militant rhetoric or political divisiveness, the articles and blog posts continually ask whether Christians can practice public engagement without becoming less human. To ask Christians to act more humanely is truly to express the desire for the Holy Spirit to sanctify God's people. The words *sanctification* and *holiness* may rarely be uttered in these conversations, but perhaps this is indicative of our deficient doctrine of the Spirit. The reason the request for greater humanity equates to a desire for sanctified people is because the Holy Spirit's work of transformation is ultimately a process of making us more and more human. It is re-humanization.

After the entry of sin into the world, humans have had little difficulty mastering the art of dehumanizing themselves and others. While not directly stated when God promises Abraham that ultimately all nations will be blessed through him (because one day the Messiah will come), part of this blessing is that those who become reunited to God through Jesus get to become proper humans again. "I'm only human" is a phrase many of us use to indicate our deficiencies and weaknesses (that is, the ways we are not perfectly human), but this is a concession to fallenness. To be Christian is to be on the way to true humanness. If Christ is the perfect human, and our aim is Christlikeness, then our goal is full humanity. Sanctification is the path and experience of moving toward this goal.

How do we get there? Christians do not have universal agreement on the process or the extent of transformation possible before the consummation of the kingdom when Christ returns. Though the Holy Spirit is a seal and deposit of our future inheritance (Ephesians 1:14), there has been much ink and paper put to use in debating how much we experience the eschatological kingdom in this life. How we answer this question is important, because it makes a tremendous difference in what kind of public practice we can expect of Christians. For example, if one believes that the Holy Spirit gives us new birth and eternal life but then only works to remind us that we are justified and belong to God, then we cannot have very high expectations of Christian behavior. Likewise, if we interpret a phrase like "purify us from all unrighteousness" (1 John 1:9) to include the fact that our salvation makes possible a state of liberation from willful sin due to the Spirit's sanctifying work, then our expectations of behavior will be very high.

Here's the way I have come to think about this: once someone is reborn as a result of the Holy Spirit's work, the process of sanctification begins. This is distinct from justification and atonement, which address our status before God as a result of Christ's crucifixion. The work of sanctification is God's gracious work to us and within us that moves us toward greater humanness. Romans 8:9 – 13 indicates this by expressing the expectation that Christians are able to be controlled by and sensitive to the work of the Holy Spirit to participate in a transformative process. Texts such as Galatians 5:13 – 26 help us see that while there is an opportunity to exhibit Christlike, fully human character, it is not easy, because of our conflict with evil desires. Christians can experience transformation, but the process may be quite uneven. Sometimes transformation happens quickly and dramatically and other times much more slowly, even imperceptibly. The fact that the process may be slow does not excuse our vices or character flaws. Rather, the call to holiness is always upon us, and we should regularly ask God to empower and change us by the Holy Spirit. Sanctification is our re-humanization by the Holy Spirit.

Public Holiness

What does it look like to be on this pathway to greater human-ness? God said "be holy because I, the LORD your God, am holy" (Leviticus 19:2) and stated multiple times that his people were to live in such a way that they were clearly distinct from others. Though Christians today are not a national people like the ancient Israelites, the call to be holy remains, just as Paul reminded the Corinthian church. In practice, our re-humanization by the Holy Spirit will manifest itself by changing our character, which is perhaps best displayed by a multifaceted expression of the second great commandment, "Love your neighbor as yourself" (Matthew 22:39). The examples I gave at the beginning of this chapter all ask what it means for Christians to live as those who truly love their neighbors. Even if one disagrees with some aspects of the specific concerns, the question is important at all levels of our relationships with others, from our interactions with "church people" to those of differing cultural and political positions. Our pursuit of holiness should not be limited to our internal transformation but should extend to all our public actions.

A word I haven't used till now, but which must be a part of this discussion, is *enemy*. Whether or not we identify any other humans (or nations) as enemies, Christians are called to exhibit love for those who in some way fit the "enemy" category (Matthew 5:44, Romans 12:17 – 21). The public discourse around political issues often has an intensity that makes it easy for "them" (anyone with an opposing view of certain important issues) to become the enemy. If we are honest, we know how easy it can be to conflate individual people with the political issues dear to them, and when those issues are ones of great tension, then that person can be seen as an enemy. It may have never been anyone's intention, but those who become political "others" because of their issues (and sometimes because of their rhetoric and behavior) morph into objects to be opposed at any cost because the stakes are high. Yet even when the stakes are high, the path of sanctification challenges us to see political opponents as neighbors, as those we must love and regard as fellow human beings.

What does it look like for people to become enemies, and what might be a model of a holy public posture? The issue of abortion is one example. This has been a longstanding political battleground (since the mid-1970s) on which some Christians have expended considerable energy and where the rhetoric and political action on both sides has sometimes gone to extremes. The issue has been framed in terms of rights, which, as Michelle Kirtley observes, has brought with it some unintended consequences directly related to the question of our public posture.

> The abortion debate has been one of the most polarizing debates in our culture in recent years, in part because many view the issue of abortion through the lens of individual rights. Indeed, a right to privacy was the basis for the Supreme Court's decision in *Roe v. Wade*. Yet this perspective of rights-based autonomy has been destructive for both supporters and opponents of abortion. Supporters claim a "right" for individual women to choose and control what happens to their own bodies, and opponents of abortion claim a "right" to life for the unborn. As a result, the rights of the unborn are pitted against the rights of women, creating a win-lose paradigm with enormous emotional stakes for all involved. Because of this

paradigm, many Christians have essentially taken sides, choosing to focus on protecting the unborn, neglecting to promote women's dignity. As a consequence, the pro-life movement and the Church by association have been quite effectively labeled as anti-woman, despite some concerted efforts to challenge this stereotype. Another troubling consequence of the rights-based paradigm is that cultural and political efforts to oppose abortion have been separated from efforts to promote women's dignity and address the many injustices women face — some of which lead women to face the awful, unwanted decision of whether or not to have an abortion.[8]

Though I doubt that the great majority of pro-life supporters are against women, it is interesting to consider the fact that many pro-choice supporters interpret the rhetoric and actions of the pro-life side as an assault on women. It may seem nonsensical to believe that the issue is about "men desiring to control women's bodies," but perhaps this is the result of rhetoric that is so focused on the unborn child that it renders the pregnant woman incidental. This may seem ridiculous, but how much evangelical discourse about abortion is focused on the woman expecting the child, apart from the consequences of choosing an abortion? Kirtley suggests a path forward:

If, instead of talking about the rights of either the unborn child or the mother, we used language of human dignity and justice, the very character of the debate might change. As Christians, our opposition to abortion is rooted in the God-given dignity of all creatures. This requires us to direct attention not only to the dignity of developing fetuses but also to their mothers, whose dignity may have been assaulted in untold ways, including those that fail to meet criminal definitions of rape. This does not mean we stop publicly opposing abortion, but it does mean that in our churches and in our political communities, we must nurture compassion that leads to action on behalf of women who face injustice.

A focus on human dignity challenges individualism in favor of a more community-based approach to the issue of unwanted pregnancy. As the Center for Public Justice Guideline says, unwanted pregnancies "call for the assumption of extraordinary responsibilities by extended family members, supportive friends and neighbors, churches, social service organizations, and/or public authorities." And in the realm of public policy, "government should do everything in the sphere of its responsibility to support adequate health care for pregnant women and for infants, encourage pregnancy counseling, promote adoption and strengthen foster care ..." it is not enough for Christians to oppose abortion. We must actively promote the dignity of women, whether that be through working to decrease maternal mortality in Africa, end sex trafficking or helping women suffering from domestic violence. In so doing, we will more accurately reflect the heart of Jesus to our fallen world.[9]

What would it mean for Christians who oppose abortion to be known as much for expressing concern about the mother as for the child? If rhetoric and practice were also reflective of our continued growth into full human beings, it would be more difficult for those in favor of a different policy to regard pro-life Christians as those who are inhumane because they are anti-woman. Try this thought experiment: What would it be like if the first thought of a woman with an unplanned pregnancy was, "I know who I can call — I can call the church, because they are committed to my well-being even if I have disagreements with them." If our public advocacy is conveyed in a manner that can present neighbor-love with the same strength as the pro-life position, our sanctification would come across in a way that would confound many. Abortion is only one example; whether areas of focus are immigration, environmental concerns, strategies for addressing poverty, or many other important issues, the call to holiness ought to profoundly shape and inform our private and public posture.

"But what about speaking the truth in a culture that is against Christ?" Surely this is the position of some conservative and progressive evangelicals who emphasize the prophetic dimension of public discourse. After all, if we are speaking the truth and find ourselves labeled as "haters," "zealots," or "those justice radicals," is this not merely akin to a contemporary experience of persecution or an emotional martyrdom? This is an important question, especially when it comes to the posture that seems to attend public discourse that emerges from a strong sense of justice or as a reaction to forms of injustice. Sanctification is not antithetical to the passionate expression of truth or even expressions of anger, but we should be hesitant to immediately associate our strong rhetorical expressions with the most pristine form of divine discourse. My point is not that we should never speak with strong passion but that we cannot forget the command to love our enemies even when we "stand for truth." Our commitment to the truth, and even our outrage at injustice and evil, are not sufficient to excuse us from remembering that even our greatest enemy should be accorded respect. To put it another way, we cannot wear the offense of others as a badge of honor because we represent truth while they do not. And perhaps we should also consider whether any pursuit of persecution or "martyrdom" in the name of truth is really more about puffing ourselves up rather than worshiping the triune God. "Holy indignation" can be one way our sanctification is expressed, but it will be discourse that identifies the truth while remaining committed to love of all neighbors.

Holiness is not supposed to be cloaked in the chambers of pious hearts but displayed in the public domains of home, school, culture, and politics. Because we continue to wait for the day that Christ sets all things in their proper order, we find the path of sanctification to be a challenge. Yet the Spirit bids us to listen to his voice and surrender to his power. If we heed this call and continue down the path of transformation, our private and public practice will produce more amazement than exasperation, and even our enemies will see that we act like those who are becoming human.

PERSEVERANCE:
STAYING IN THE GAME

N OT GUILTY."

Though George Zimmerman was expressionless when he heard these words on July 13, 2013, he no doubt felt as though he could finally exhale. February 26, 2012, was the rainy night when George Zimmerman, a Hispanic neighborhood watch coordinator, fatally shot seventeen-year-old Trayvon Martin, a young man who was unarmed — and African American. Zimmerman had not been initially arrested because the initial investigation did not dispute his claim that the shooting happened in self-defense. The story became public and generated considerable media coverage (including some misleading stories), and there was a public outcry for a larger investigation and Zimmerman's arrest. I wasn't sure what to think about the case, though it was hard not to wonder how much this incident was connected to debates about racial profiling. Six weeks after the incident, Zimmerman was arrested, and his case went to trial in June 2013.

While Zimmerman exhaled upon the utterance of his acquittal, many others felt distressed and exasperated, because to them the verdict represented ongoing systemic injustice for African Americans. Other observers felt differently about the verdict, seeing it as the only possible verdict based on the evidence — and they were also certain that the trial had nothing to do with race. The days and weeks following the verdict saw much discussion of the trial and the state of race in the United States; television, magazines, news outlets, and the blogosphere were full of stories and opinions about the court proceedings and various aspects of race relations in the United States, There were even marches and rallies to protest the verdict. I found it impossible to ignore the furor, and I wasn't completely sure what to think about what I was reading and hearing. In many cases, the people who expressed anger conveyed perplexity that others did not see things as clearly as they did. Wasn't it obvious that the Martin/Zimmerman incident and trial were about race? Or wasn't it obvious that this was a tragic event, but it occurred in the course of self-defense? I found myself in emotional turmoil at times because so much rhetoric was full of passion and conviction, yet there was little forward momentum toward the kind of deep, complex understanding that would help us to move toward a more whole society. While there was some insightful and clear-headed commentary to be found amidst the uproar, the intensity of the public conversation made one thing clear: though the United States is a more than a hundred and fifty years past the Emancipation Proclamation and nearly fifty years past the landmark civil rights legislation of 1964 and 1965, there is much that remains to be done to resolve the issue of race.

While none of us can question that we are in a different place than we were even forty years ago, the reaction to the Zimmerman verdict made it clear that we have not come nearly as far as we might think. This is less because of those who continue to make racism a matter of conviction or even virtue, but due more to the subtle and invisible ways that the legacy of race continues to work against the possibility of a society that is truly equal and promotes the flourishing of all human beings.

Could things be worse? That's the wrong question in a broken world where it is easy to find depressing and horrific stories of all kinds. For Christians committed to cultural engagement and public responsibility, we have to continually pursue those things that make the world better. Yet as the lingering challenge of race reveals, the change we hope for often happens more slowly than we would like. I can personally feel the inertia.

This is hardly limited to the United States. One of my former students has worked in Africa on a number of occasions and has found himself perplexed with the way that humanitarian aid and development works out on the ground. I asked him to put his experience into words:

> Though my experience is still limited, I've seen enough in my several years living and working with both governmental and nongovernmental aid and development programs in West and Central Africa to have ample reason to be discouraged. When well-intentioned compassion lacks sufficient grounding, it can be disastrous. When well-founded programs become self-sustaining power struggles, it is debilitating. And when Christians continue to uncritically conform to the ideals of humanitarianism, it is disorienting. One project that I managed provided emergency food assistance to people who had recently been displaced by war. When I discovered that the governmental group

funding this project, local officials, and beneficiary representatives had schemed together to sell hundreds of tons of food in local markets (and that this was the norm!), I was devastated. This influx of food dropped market prices and crippled the local farmers who were trying to sell their products in this same market. Over years, it had led many farmers to abandon their fields. What do we do when the same governments that coordinate and fund most humanitarian aid are linked to the causes of the chronic problems for which their aid is intended? What do we do when we realize that massive influxes of resources and leadership inhibits indigenous productive dignity, and when there seem to be so many more problems with engagement than with disengagement?

In the last decade or two there has been a greater emphasis on Christian public action focused on addressing problems linked to global poverty and development. Whether due to tragic consequences of colonialism, differing rates of development, natural disasters, drought, corrupt governments, or even some effects of globalization, multiple issues must be addressed, from disease to clean water to economic growth. Many Christians are passionate about some form of advocacy for or participation in the processes of development. Yet as the above quote reveals, humanitarian assistance and development are slow, complex, and often perplexing fields. In my own experiences in developing countries, I have found myself asking "How is change possible?" "Where do we begin?" and "What does it take to create a pathway to flourishing?" I vividly remember awaking in the middle of the night in Uganda with my mind racing as I wondered how long-lasting transformation could happen. I was well aware that I would only be there briefly before returning to the United States, while the residents I met faced a daily existence full of challenges.

The changes we hope for in society are not the only ones that occur. Just as there are changes that do not happen quickly enough, others happen more quickly than we would wish, and some we wish would not happen at all. One example is what we might call the "success" of the sexual revolution. While we could say it is more of a catastrophe than a success, because of the relational carnage on display in our culture, the fact remains that we are a more sexually permissive society, and this permissiveness has even permeated into the church, perhaps most consequentially in the increase in cohabitation and the culture of divorce. Of course, the sexual revolution is not the only factor in the modern crisis of marriage, but it plays a prominent role. One of the most serious implications of the success of this revolution is that marriage rates have declined in general, but more notably among the lower middle class on down, though couples continue to have children outside of marriage.[10] The instability of the relationships among the parents plays a significant role in reducing the chances of later success in life for these children,[11] which ultimately contributes to an ongoing crisis for society, one that calls for various public strategies. Though we may often think of the sexual revolution as a mere cultural phenomenon that celebrates the experience of sensual pleasures, the revolution's success has reverberated in society in ways that have yielded great social and political challenges. As one of my colleagues in political science put it, "As a result of this greater reduction in marriage among those in the lower classes, we are on the way to becoming Argentina." (Translation: There is a large and widening gap between the rich and poor). Such changes in society can frustrate us as much as the slow path toward the types of sociopolitical change we hope for.

Facing Our Distress

What should we do in light of this frustration? Is it time to heed the call for an end to culture wars and attempts to bring about social transformation through political means? James Davison Hunter's *To Change the World* (2010) generated a lot of conversation on this question. Hunter, a University of Virginia sociologist, argued that many contemporary Christians misunderstand the means and process of social change, particularly those who primarily pursue this change via politics. Though I have my concerns with Hunter's book,[12] one of its most helpful aspects was the section that revealed that most changes in society take place much more slowly than we recognize and rarely, for example, in the span of a generation.[13] Hunter was one notable voice calling for a strategy with less attention to success in political battles and more emphasis on Christlike faithfulness in our smaller spheres of influence. He is not alone. Before and since the publication of Hunter's book, some have called for a retreat from political engagement because there have been minimal gains. There are others who have not wanted to disengage but have wondered what alternative path to pursue in politics or other forms of public action.

Irrespective of the different responses, the common frustration about the slow pace of change reveals an important theological truth: the echoes of the fall are all around us and routinely sabotage our best intentions, whether personal or public and political. Like unwelcome waves on our shores, the stubborn persistence of race, the twisted trajectories of humanitarian action, and the socially catastrophic success of the sexual revolution are only a few examples of a broken world resistant to positive change. And we need to be clear that sin is far more than personal; it has structural manifestations that leave evil in place or introduce it anew in public life.

Though positive change has happened in the past and may happen in the future, we must face the harsh truth that we cannot easily manage the direction of society (even if we gain lots of power), and that we cannot always discern the best path toward a good society. History is not a ship easily guided by our grand plans and dreams. Something always seems to happen to frustrate the process. For some of us, when we face all the evidence of dysfunction and resistance to social change, we might find ourselves wondering if we are simply helpless, subject to the whims of history and hardly more than passengers as the ship takes its unpredictable course. Even those most optimistic among us have to admit that frustration and messiness will always be the companion of our transformative strategies. Resistance is before us at every step.

What do we do with the reality of frustration? If we look at the lives of nations and observe that each advance seems to be matched by an incidence of resistance, or if we find ourselves desperately in search of any harbinger of positive change, how do we resist the temptation to leave the game of public engagement and put ourselves on the bench permanently? Chapter one makes clear that I am convinced that public responsibility is important for Christians. Thus, returning to the bench does not seem like the best or most faithful option. Still, it is important to acknowledge that the frustrations characterized by the examples at the beginning of this chapter are real and create a tension with the Christian opportunity and responsibility for public engagement. It would be a mistake to say simply that we should charge ahead with ultimate victory in view as if the proper response is to double down on our public mission. We have to face the distress that comes with public participation. It is important to tell the truth about it and then consider how to keep going forward. We must ask how we as Christians manage to live in the era between Christ's ascension and his return to bring an end to history. At this time in history, we routinely encounter reminders that while we have a taste of God's kingdom in the present, we do not have it at full strength. We need to seriously consider ways to be truthful and faithful as we experience the tension that comes with our in-between-times territory.

Truth and Lament

There are three areas that I will consider here.

The first is what some call the long-lost art of lament. Though I have encountered many Christians who have mourned in the face of loss and tragedy, the practice of lament has been a relatively new dimension to my conversations with God. I propose the practice of lament in the face of the frustrations that attend the practice of public engagement because this is a way for Christians to fiercely tell the truth about the heartbreak the world brings to us. The book of Lamentations and the Psalms provide us with great examples of God's people telling the truth about the disappointments of life, whether self-inflicted like the exile of the people of Judah or because of the harsh circumstances of life. There is no effort to escape the harshness of truth in words such as these:

I am overwhelmed with troubles
and my life draws near to death.
I am counted among those who go down to the pit;
I am like one without strength.
I am set apart with the dead,
like the slain who lie in the grave,
whom you remember no more,
who are cut off from your care.

(Psalm 88: 3 – 5)

My eyes fail from weeping,
I am in torment within;
my heart is poured out on the ground
because my people are destroyed,
because children and infants faint
in the streets of the city.

They say to their mothers,
"Where is bread and wine?"
as they faint like the wounded
in the streets of the city,
as their lives ebb away
in their mothers' arms.

(Lamentations 2:11 – 12)

These texts cry out to God, sometimes in complaint and sometimes in mourning, but always zealously telling the truth about the horrors of personal darkness and exile. This should also be the path we take in light of frustrating situations like the ones above. In the face of the reactions to Trayvon Martin's death along with the trial and subsequent acquittal of George Zimmerman, perhaps we should cry out to God in grief that a young man has met an early death (regardless of whether we regard him as an innocent victim or not) and that many others meet a similar demise. Whatever we believe about Zimmerman, might we not also lament that he not only shot someone but will have to live with the fact of taking a young man's life? Beyond Martin and Zimmerman, do we cry out to God because we live in a world where racism and ethnocentrism still exist and affect the lives of many people? Do we lament the inability of people (including Christians) to constructively discuss and consider the many problems in our society that touch on race in some way? And what lament might we offer in the face of humanitarian practices that seem to harm those it intends to help? Do we mourn not only the distressed life circumstances of those who live in circumstances such as abject poverty but also the corruption linked to the exchange of power and money? Is there a lament for a society where marriage is in a state of crisis, especially among those who are poorer?

The practice of lament helps us tell the truth about the frustration that attends public responsibility. We can admit that we get exhausted and exasperated at the resistance to positive change, and we can come to God with brutal honesty when our hearts break in the face of what we see. But the practice of lament is not a commitment to hiding in our prayer closet until Jesus returns. To lament means we participate in an ongoing practice of putting our disappointments in God's hands, including the times when we are tempted to get out of the game. Yet it is as important to stay in the game of public responsibility as it is to pursue our internal transformation into Christlikeness. Lament helps us to own our frustration without quitting.

Tempering Expectations

A second important area is our view of history. This is really a question of the way we understand our responsibilities in the world in relationship to the way God will bring about the end of history. Are we merely spectators to history? Or do we have a role to play in establishing God's kingdom? Do we set aside any expectations and simply make the best of it? We can see one interesting example in the decades before the Civil War in the United States. Back then there were many who held to a post-millennial eschatology that influenced Christian public action. Generally speaking, postmillennial eschatology is a view that says Jesus will return after the millennial reign described in Revelation 20:1 – 6. Many postmillennialists in the seventeen and eighteen hundreds were convinced that it was their Christian responsibility to usher in the kingdom of God by preaching and teaching. For some this led to socially transformative efforts such as the Temperance Movement and Women's Suffrage Movement. The hope was that ultimately there would be a great revival, which would lead to the conversion of many people before Christ returned. We can look back and see that, though there may have been some social progress, we still await the great world transformation and Christ's return.

After the Civil War — a terrible chapter of United States history that devastated optimism — postmillennialism eventually fell out of favor, and a more negative view of the trajectory of history gained favor among evangelical Christians. If we take a long look at history, we see that peaks and valleys are all around. There have been great revolutions and terrible social ills, and Christians have had positive and negative views of the role we play in history up to this day.

What should be our perspective? Here's one way to look at it: Whether we are reading about Jesus's description of the end in Matthew 24 – 25, Paul's words in 1 Thessalonians 4 – 5, Peter's words in 2 Peter 3, or John's words in Revelation 20 – 22, we see the common thread that God will be the one who ultimately finishes the story. In the meantime, it is our task to trust God to bring about the final end without confusing our imperfect efforts with his closing act. What this means in terms of history is that we should refrain from both excessive pessimism and excessive optimism when it comes to our actions in the public realm. This leads us to have an approach to society where we are committed to transformation without putting pressure on ourselves to usher in the ultimate triumph.

This does not mean we have no contribution to make to history, but it helps us temper our expectations with humility. The point is not that we should never usher a call to action for a particular objective, but that we ought to pause before challenging fellow Christians to be the special generation that makes a unique mark on history. Of course it is quite possible that there might be special persons or special groups of people whose words and deeds have a uniquely transformative impact on the direction of society, but we should be cautious about the language that we use and refrain from grand predictions. This is particularly important in light of the inevitable frustrations that will emerge once rhetoric is followed by concrete actions. The road to change tends to be longer than we expect and may often take detours we never anticipated. This caution should not lead us to avoid engagement, but to resist the triumphalist temptation that can lead to false expectations of success, as if our vision and strategy was hand delivered by a divine emissary.

Humility does not mean our actions are insignificant but rather that they can never be regarded as the ultimate acts of history that fix the deepest problems of the world. We may make significant contributions to the state of marriage and contribute to the flourishing of the poor, but we will not make the kingdom of God arrive in its fullness by our participation in society. Instead, we are able to be faithful in our public responsibility in the face of lingering frustrations with the process of transformation. We hope for our actions to make a difference, but we remember that our progress does not write the final chapter of history. Neither our actions nor the resistance that frustrates us has the final word.

Suffering along the Way

The third area follows from a commitment to humble transformation. If we are honest about the fact that change takes a long time and that frustrations can be so great that our hearts break, we will acknowledge that suffering is a normal part of engagement in public responsibility. If we take this dimension of suffering seriously, it will lead us to make an important modification to the way we talk about public engagement. We should still use the word *transformation*, but we must modify it so that it reflects the reality of suffering. I propose the label *cruciform transformation* to convey this perspective. The label *cruciform* is not intended to suggest that our public actions contribute to our salvation but that the path of public engagement may include great suffering on the part of those who are pursuing the common good of society. Though we may often think of following Jesus as a matter of our personal piety, the path of cross-bearing extends to all the acts that we do as Christians, including the practice of public engagement. To bear the cross is not to suggest that we are always defeated but that we may indeed encounter great anguish as we pursue a better world.

Cruciform transformation does not mean that every act of public engagement is guaranteed to produce a level of suffering that amounts to personal or collective cross-bearing, but it does help us to be honest about the great difficulties that might occur. If we consider the kind of suffering that many people experience around the world when they pursue a more equal or just society, we quickly become aware that there is often a heavy price to be paid for social transformation. Some people pay with their lives, some suffer a heavy emotional toll, and some people have less visible forms of suffering. For Christians who suffer in these circumstances, the suffering is not necessarily or primarily due to persecution for their identification with Christ but likely more due to the pursuit of justice. This pursuit flows from the belief that we serve a God who himself is the standard for justice, though that belief may not be explicitly stated.

The contribution of a cruciform-transformation perspective is that it can help us to be courageous and realistic as we seek to honor God by remaining faithful to the task of public engagement. Those who travel the winding road of change in society may also have to stop at clinics and hospitals to have their wounds washed and bound, and others may need to talk with someone to help them process horrors they encounter on the way. But they stay on the path toward transformation. If Christians desire to participate in processes such as undoing the damage of racism and crafting alternative paths to humanitarian practice in developing countries, frustration and pain are sure to be present. For some, the experience may be like that of martyrdom, while for others it may simply be perplexing and exhausting. But these people stay in the game, not even looking at the bench.

In the end, the reason for staying in the game is the same reason for getting into it in the first place. God gave humans a Great Commission and never rescinded it. Though we live after Christ's incarnation and the first installment of his kingdom, the brokenness in the world that has been "normal" since Genesis 3 still threatens our efforts at all times. We experience the ongoing reverberations of the fall in all dimensions of life, and when these reverberations appear in society, it can be scary, frustrating, exhausting, distressing — the list goes on. The great temptation many of us face today is to leave the mess of the public square and find another way to be faithful, a way that may be less costly though maybe less spiritually valuable. To yield to such a temptation is to develop amnesia about our first commandment and commission. Lament, humility, and a cruciform perspective help us to stay with our task in the face of frustration. The public thorns, thistles, and weeds that spring up as we sow seeds in public life are truly a bother, but we must press forward in public faithfulness. Perseverance is not easy, but our public responsibility beckons.

POSTSCRIPT

OUR BELIEFS MATTER

IN THIS BRIEF BOOK, MY ULTIMATE AIM HAS BEEN TO CONsider how some of our Christian beliefs lead us toward a practice of public faithfulness. In teaching courses on political theology, one of the interesting issues I have had to consider is the public impact of our doctrines, even when such impacts may be unintentional. We each have to ask ourselves an important question when we consider the whole of our Christian beliefs altogether: What difference do my beliefs make for the world around me?

I am reminded of a question that haunted the late German theologian Dorothy Soelle when she reflected on growing up during the time of the Holocaust. She wondered, "Didn't you smell the gas?" as she thought about the beliefs of those in the church who seemed to sit by while disaster befell so many Jewish people. Her question leads me to ask what kinds of things we allow to occur in our society even as we regard ourselves as faithful people who worship God and aim to follow his Word. What do our beliefs make possible, and what do they leave in place? It is a hard question for us to face, but for those who regard themselves as people of the Book, we have to consider whether we really practice our faith in a way that reflects the full depth of truth in the Bible.

I have had conversations with people who have become convinced that the approach to the Bible and faith taken by evangelicals is unable to facilitate practices of justice. I am not convinced of this view, but I wonder what dimensions of our faith remain to be articulated and put in practice. For instance, what dimensions of our doctrines do we need to understand and put into practice in order for evangelicals to lead the way in addressing the thorny issues of race? What might we be missing in our faith that leads us to evangelize around the world while struggling to give attention to the complexities of social, economic, and political development?

To those reading this book, I ask you to consider where your beliefs take you and where your beliefs might be under-developed. There are, for example, great public implications for the full range of our doctrines of creation, Christology, and ecclesiology. How have you put together the story of your faith, and where does the story go once your faith makes its way into the world beyond the church, the world beyond Sunday? The doctrines we believe have great potential impact for the world around us. We have before us the opportunity to grow deeper in our knowledge of God and more faithful as disciples of Christ. Our beliefs are not only for our personal gain but also for public expression. May we be those who not only profess that we are witnesses to the kingdom of God but also those whose lives reveal that we are growing ever more deeply in our understanding and practice of the mission God has given us.

NOTES

1. John MacKay, *A Preface to Christian Theology* (New York: Macmillan, 1941), 27.

2. Abraham Kuyper, *Lectures on Calvinism* (Grand Rapids: Eerdmans, 1931), 30.

3. Vincent Bacote, *The Spirit in Public Theology: Appropriating the Legacy of Abraham Kuyper* (Grand Rapids: Baker Academic, 2005), 7.

4. See Michael Horton, *The Christian Faith: A Systematic Theology for Pilgrims on the Way* (Grand Rapids: Zondervan, 2011), 379 – 407.

5. Sarah Pulliam Bailey, "Q&A: Anne Rice on Following Christ without Christianity," *Christianity Today*, August 17, 2010, http://www.christianity today.com/ct/2010/augustweb-only/43-21.0.html.

6. Rachel Held Evans, "How to Win a Culture War and Lose a Generation," personal blog, http://rachelheldevans.com/blog/win-culture-war-lose -generation-amendment-one-north-carolina#.

7. David Kinnaman and Gabe Lyons, *unChristian: What a New Generation Really Thinks about Christianity ... and Why It Matters* (Grand Rapids: Baker, 2007), 34.

8. Michelle Crotwell Kirtley, "Rising Above the Rights-Based Abortion Debate," *Capital Commentary*, August 31, 2012, http://www.capital commentary.org/abortion/rising-above-rights-based-abortion-debate.

9. Ibid.

10. "Social Indicators of Marital Health and Well-Being: Trends of the Past Five Decades," *The State of Our Unions* website, http://www.state ofourunions.org/2011/social_indicators.php#marriage.

11. "Beyond the economic advantages of marriage for the married couples themselves, marriage has a tremendous economic impact on society. Marriage trends have a big impact on family income levels and inequality. After more than doubling between 1947 and 1977, the growth of median family income has slowed in recent years. A major reason is that married couples, who fare better economically than their single counterparts, have been a rapidly decreasing proportion of total families. In this same twenty-year period, and in large part because of changes in family structure, family income inequality has significantly increased. Research has consistently shown that divorce and unmarried childbearing increase child poverty. In recent years the majority of children who grow up outside of married families have experienced at least one year of dire poverty. According to one study, if family structure had not changed between 1960 and 1998, the black child poverty rate in 1998 would have been 28.4 percent rather than 45.6 percent, and the white child poverty rate would have been 11.4 percent rather than 15.4 percent.

"The rise in child poverty, of course, generates significant public costs in health and welfare programs." See Adam Thomas and Isabel Sawhill, "For Richer or for Poorer: Marriage as an Antipoverty Strategy," *Journal of Policy Analysis and Management* 21 (2002): 587 – 99.

12. See Vincent Bacote, "Beyond Faithful Presence: Abraham Kuyper's Legacy for Common Grace and Cultural Development," *Journal of Markets and Morality* 16, no. 1 (Spring 2013): 195 – 205.

13. See James Davison Hunter, *To Change the World: The Irony, Tragedy, and Possibility of Christianity in the Late Modern World* (New York: Oxford University Press, 2010), 32 – 78.

Ordinary Theology

Scalpel and the Cross

A Theology of Surgery

Gene L. Green

We know the bedrock themes upon which the Christian faith stands: creation, fall, redemption, restoration. As Christians, we live within these great moments of God's plan for humanity and all of his creation. In other words, our lives are part of Christian theology—every part of our lives, even surgery.

As a part of Zondervan's Ordinary Theology Series, *The Scalpel and the Cross* recounts New Testament professor Gene Green's encounter with open-heart surgery and carefully examines the many ways in which Christian doctrine spoke into the experience. The result is a short book that avoids shallow explanations and glib promises, instead guiding readers to a deeper understanding and an enduring hope in the face of one of modern life's necessary traumas.

Available in stores and online!

Ordinary Theology

Cities of Tomorrow and the City to Come

A Theology of Urban Life

Noah J. Toly
Gene L. Green, Series Editor

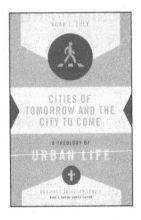

Each day, the world's urban population swells by almost 200,000. With every passing week, more than a million people new to cities face unexpected realities and challenges of urban life. Just like the sheer volume of people in the city, these challenges can be staggering. As with the height and breadth of our metropolises, the wonders of urban life can be breathtaking. Like the city itself, the questions and challenges of urban life are both sprawling and pulsing with vitality..

As part of Zondervan's Ordinary Theology Series, this volume offers a series of Christian reflections on some of the most basic and universal challenges of 21st century urban life. It takes one important dimension of what it means to be human—that human beings are made to be for God, for others, and for creation—and asks, "What are the implications of who God made us to be for how we ought to live in our cities?"

This book is intended for Christians facing the riddle of urban creation care, discerning the shape of community life, struggling with the challenges of wealth and poverty, and wondering at the global influence of cities. It is meant for those whose lives and livelihoods are inextricably bound up in the flourishing of their neighborhood and also for those who live in the shadow of cities. Most of all, it is meant for those grappling with the relationship between the cities of tomorrow and the glorious city to come.

Available in stores and online!

Ordinary Theology

Faithful

A Theology of Sex

Beth Felker Jones
Gene L. Green, Series Editor

Many believers accept traditional Christian
sexual morality but have very little idea why it
matters for the Christian life. In *Faithful*, author
Beth Felker Jones sketches a theology of sexuality that demonstrates sex is not about legalis-
tic morals with no basis in reality but rather about the God who is faithful
to us.

In Hosea 2:19–20 God says to Israel, "I will take you for my wife forever;
I will take you for my wife in righteousness and in justice, in steadfast love,
and in mercy. I will take you for my wife in faithfulness; and you shall know
the Lord." This short book explores the goodness of sexuality as created
and redeemed, and it suggests ways to navigate the difficulties of living in a
world in which sexuality, like everything else, suffers the effects of the fall.

As part of Zondervan's Ordinary Theology Series, *Faithful* takes
a deeper look at a subject Christians talk about often but not always
thoughtfully. This short, insightful reflection explores the deeper significance of the body and sexuality.

Available in stores and online!